Presented to

_____

by _____

on _____

Why Is There
a Cross?

Kathleen Long Bostrom
Illustrated by Elena Kucharik

Tyndale House Publishers, Inc.
WHEATON, ILLINOIS

Visit Tyndale's exciting Web site at www.tyndale.com

TYNDALE is a registered trademark of Tyndale House Publishers, Inc.
Tyndale Kids logo is a trademark of Tyndale House Publishers, Inc.

Little Blessings is a registered trademark of Tyndale House Publishers, Inc.
The Little Blessings characters are a trademark of Elena Kucharik.

Why Is There a Cross?

Edited by Betty Free Swanberg
Designed by Catherine Bergstrom

Scripture quotations are taken from the *Holy Bible,* New Living Translation, copyright ©
1996, 2004. Used by permission of Tyndale House Publishers, Inc., Wheaton, Illinois 60189.
All rights reserved.

Library of Congress Cataloging-in-Publication Data

Bostrom, Kathleen Long.
   Why is there a cross? / Kathleen Long Bostrom ; illustrated by Elena Kucharik.
      p. cm. — (Little blessings)
   ISBN-13: 978-1-4143-0288-1 (hardcover)
   ISBN-10: 1-4143-0288-6 (hardcover)
   1. Jesus Christ—Crucifixion—Juvenile literature. I. Kucharik, Elena. II. Title. III. Little
   blessings picture books.
   BT453.B68 2005
   232.96—dc22   2004030752

Printed in Singapore

12 11 10 09 08 07 06
7   6   5   4   3   2   1

To Peggy Callison, my lifelong friend
and friend for life.
With love always,
Kathy

To my grandson, Max.
With love,
Elena

When I am in church

and I look all around,

I always try hard

not to make any sound.

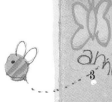

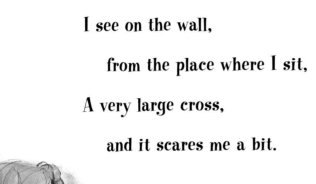

I see on the wall,

    from the place where I sit,

A very large cross,

    and it scares me a bit.

I know that when Jesus

was ready to die,

He died on a cross,

but I'm wondering, *Why?*

What did he do

that was so very wrong?

Why couldn't everyone

just get along?

Did Jesus feel sad?

Do you think he was scared?

I wonder, *Did Jesus*

think nobody cared?

Why did his life

    have to turn out this way?

Could Jesus have changed it

    by running away?

How can I manage

to do my own part

To show I love Jesus

with all of my heart?

You're wanting to know

what the cross is about?
It isn't so easy

to figure it out.

Let's look through the Bible,

for then we will see
Why the cross is important

to you and to me.

The crosses we see—

    both the large and the small—

Remind us that Christ

    gave his life for us all.

19

His death on the cross

was a part of the plan

That God had in mind

when Creation began.

Although we may struggle

with all of our might,

There's simply no way

we will always do right.

Jesus was willing

to die for our sin.

He gave up his life

so that we can all win!

Jesus is perfect—

as good as can be.

He went to the cross

so that we could be free:

Free from the power

of sin and of death;

Free to praise Jesus

with every breath.

Even though Jesus

   did just what God asked,

Facing the cross

   was a difficult task.

A-Z

Just before Jesus

was taken away,

He went to a garden

and knelt down to pray.

He said with great sadness,

"Dear God, help me through.

You know that I'll do

what you ask me to do."

Jesus could face, then,

what had to be done.

He knew that God loved him,

for he is God's Son.

He went to the cross:

On Good Friday he died.

A few of his friends

were right there by his side.

Although it is sad

that our Lord had to die,

Christ rose from the dead,

and that isn't a lie!

Because Jesus lives,

we can share in his glory,

And this is the truth

of the whole Easter story!

The cross, which was once

such a terrible sight,

Now shines with the beauty

of God's holy light.

If you trust in Jesus

and give him your best,

You'll show that you love him,

and you will be blessed.

Nothing can keep you

apart from God's love;

No, nothing on earth

or in heaven above.

Death cannot stop it,

not worry or fear.

God's love is forever,

so be of good cheer!

Bible References

The answers in this poem come from God's Word. Talking about these Bible verses with your child will help your little one begin to understand that the Bible answers all of our questions about the cross. You may want to open your Bible and show your child where these verses can be found.

**The crosses we see—both the large and the small—
Remind us that Christ gave his life for us all.**

> He personally carried our sins in his body on the cross. 1 PETER 2:24

> We know what real love is because Jesus gave up his life for us. 1 JOHN 3:16

**His death on the cross was a part of the plan
That God had in mind when Creation began.**

> God chose [Christ] as your ransom long before the world began. 1 PETER 1:20

**Although we may struggle with all of our might,
There's simply no way we will always do right.**

> Everyone has sinned. ROMANS 3:23

> I want to do what is good, but I don't. I don't want to do what is wrong, but I do it anyway. But if I do what I don't want to do, I am not really the one doing wrong; it is sin living in me that does it. ROMANS 7:19-20

**Jesus was willing to die for our sin.
He gave up his life so that we can all win!**

> [Jesus said,] "Don't you realize that I could ask my Father for thousands of angels to protect us, and he would send them instantly? But if I did, how would the Scriptures be fulfilled that describe what must happen now?" MATTHEW 26:53-54

> God . . . forgave all our sins. He canceled the record of the charges against us and took it away by nailing it to the cross. COLOSSIANS 2:13-14

Jesus is perfect—as good as can be.

> [Jesus] is able, once and forever, to save those who come to God through him. He . . . is holy and blameless, unstained by sin. HEBREWS 7:25-26

> [Jesus] never sinned. 1 PETER 2:22

He went to the cross so that we could be free:

**Free from the power of sin and of death;
Free to praise Jesus with every breath.**

> Our old sinful selves were crucified with Christ so that sin might lose its power in our lives. ROMANS 6:6

> Now you are free from . . . sin. ROMANS 6:18

> I will praise the LORD at all times. I will constantly speak his praises. PSALM 34:1

Even though Jesus did just what God asked,
Facing the cross was a difficult task.

> He became anguished and distressed. . . . "My soul is crushed with grief." MATTHEW 26:37-38

Just before Jesus was taken away,
He went to a garden and knelt down to pray.

> Jesus went with [his disciples] to the olive grove called Gethsemane, and he said, "Sit here while I go over there to pray." MATTHEW 26:36

He said with great sadness, "Dear God, help me through.
You know that I'll do what you ask me to do."

> "Abba, Father," [Jesus] cried out, "everything is possible for you. Please take this cup of suffering away from me. Yet I want your will to be done, not mine." MARK 14:36

He went to the cross: On Good Friday he died.
A few of his friends were right there by his side.

> Standing near the cross were Jesus' mother, and his mother's sister, Mary (the wife of Clopas), and Mary Magdalene. When Jesus saw his mother standing there beside the disciple he loved, he said to her, "Dear woman, here is your son." And he said to [John], "Here is your mother." JOHN 19:25-27

> [Jesus] said, "It is finished!" Then he bowed his head and released his spirit. JOHN 19:30

Although it is sad that our Lord had to die,
Christ rose from the dead, and that isn't a lie!

Then the angel spoke to the women. "Don't be afraid!" he said. "I know you are looking for Jesus, who was crucified. He isn't here! He is risen from the dead, just as he said would happen. Come, see where his body was lying." MATTHEW 28:5-6

God released [Jesus] from the horrors of death and raised him back to life, for death could not keep him in its grip. ACTS 2:24

Because Jesus lives, we can share in his glory,
And this is the truth of the whole Easter story!

Through the death of Christ . . . [God] has brought you into his own presence, and you are holy and blameless as you stand before him without a single fault. COLOSSIANS 1:22

We are made right with God by placing our faith in Jesus Christ. And this is true for everyone who believes, no matter who we are. ROMANS 3:22

The cross, which was once such a terrible sight,
Now shines with the beauty of God's holy light.

Because of the joy awaiting him, [Jesus] endured the cross, disregarding its shame. Now he is seated in the place of honor beside God's throne. HEBREWS 12:2

If you trust in Jesus and give him your best,
You'll show that you love him, and you will be blessed.

> [Jesus said,] "Trust in God, and trust also in me. . . . All who love me will do what I say. My Father will love them, and we will come and make our home with each of them." JOHN 14:1, 23

Nothing can keep you apart from God's love;
No, nothing on earth or in heaven above.

> No power in the sky above or in the earth below—indeed, nothing in all creation will ever be able to separate us from the love of God that is revealed in Christ Jesus our Lord. ROMANS 8:39

Death cannot stop it, not worry or fear.
God's love is forever, so be of good cheer!

> [Jesus said,] "Be sure of this: I am with you always, even to the end of the age." MATTHEW 28:20

> I am convinced that nothing can ever separate us from God's love. Neither death nor life . . . neither our fears for today nor our worries about tomorrow . . . can separate us from God's love. ROMANS 8:38

About the Author

Kathleen Long Bostrom is the author of eight Little Blessings books and nearly two dozen other books for children. The poetic questions in her books are based on actual questions from "little blessings" she has known. Kathy is an award-winning preacher and writer, and is frequently asked to speak at conferences on Christian writing and publishing.

Kathy earned a doctor of ministry in preaching degree from McCormick Theological Seminary in Chicago, Illinois, and a master of arts in Christian education and a master of divinity degree from Princeton Theological Seminary. She also received a bachelor of arts degree in psychology from California State University, Long Beach, California.

Kathy and her husband, Greg, live with their three children—Christopher, Amy, and David—in Wildwood, Illinois. Kathy and Greg serve as co-pastors of Wildwood Presbyterian Church.

Kathy hopes that her books will be used not only with parents and children but also in Sunday school classes, preschools, and church worship settings.

About the Illustrator

Elena Kucharik, well-known Care Bears artist, has created the Little Blessings characters that appear in the line of Little Blessings products for young children and their families.

Born in Cleveland, Ohio, Elena received a bachelor of fine arts degree in commercial art at Kent State University. After graduation she worked as a greeting card artist and art director at American Greetings Corporation in Cleveland.

For more than 25 years Elena has been a freelance illustrator. During this time she was the lead artist and developer of Care Bears, as well as a designer and illustrator for major corporations and publishers. For over 10 years Elena has been focusing her talents on illustrations for children's books.

Elena and her husband live in Madison, Connecticut, and have two grown daughters.

Books in the Little Blessings Line